Young Writers 2006

'I ha
childre
where
color c
of their character.'

Martin Luther King

I have a dream
words to change the world

- MOTIVATE your pupils to write and appreciate poetry.
- INSPIRE them to share their hopes and dreams for the future.
- BOOST awareness of your school's creative ability.
- WORK alongside the National Curriculum or the high level National Qualification Skills.
- Supports the *Every Child Matters - Make a Positive Contribution* outcome.
- Over £7,000 of great prizes for schools and pupils.

'When I was out there I was never ever alone, there was always a team of people behind me, in mind if not in body.'
Ellen MacArthur

CW00369121

North East & North West England Vol II
Edited by Heather Killingray

 Young**Writers**

First published in Great Britain in 2006 by:
Young Writers
Remus House
Coltsfoot Drive
Peterborough
PE2 9JX
Telephone: 01733 890066
Website: www.youngwriters.co.uk

SB ISBN 1 84602 665 2

Foreword

Imagine a teenager's brain; a fertile yet fragile expanse teeming with ideas, aspirations, questions and emotions. Imagine a classroom full of racing minds, scratching pens writing an endless stream of ideas and thoughts . . .

. . . Imagine your words in print reaching a wider audience. Imagine that maybe, just maybe, your words can make a difference. Strike a chord. Touch a life. Change the world. Imagine no more . . .

'I Have a Dream' is a series of poetry collections written by 11 to 18-year-olds from schools and colleges across the UK and overseas. Pupils were invited to send us their poems using the theme 'I Have a Dream'. Selected entries range from dreams they've experienced to childhood fantasies of stardom and wealth, through inspirational poems of their dreams for a better future and of people who have influenced and inspired their lives.

The series is a snapshot of who and what inspires, influences and enthuses young adults of today. It shows an insight into their hopes, dreams and aspirations of the future and displays how their dreams are an escape from the pressures of today's modern life. Young Writers are proud to present this anthology, which is truly inspired and sure to be an inspiration to all who read it.

Contents

Park High School, Birkenhead

Jake Scott (12)	114
Kurtis Sinnett (13)	115
Graham Stringfellow (13)	116
Grace Dodd (12)	117
Aaron Dodd (12)	118
Abigail Evans (12)	119
Steven Gateley (12)	120
Tyler Neill (13)	121
Katrina Bimpson (13)	122
Hannah Shaw (12)	123
Nicole Carty (13)	124
Rachel Bardullas (13)	125
Camille Brougham (13)	126
Sarah Guntrip (13)	127
Chris James-Parr (13)	128
Jessica Ferguson (13)	129
Jamie Francis (14)	130
Nathan Standing (13)	131
Becky Taylor (13)	132
Hollie Rugen (13)	133
John Bilton (13)	134
Kayleigh Brabander (13)	135
Ben Redfern (13)	136
Jonathan Williams (13)	137
Emma Williams (13)	138
Andy McNally	139
Conor Walker (13)	140
Kerry Keane (14)	141
Katie Wilson (14)	142
Daniel Rainford (13)	143
Stephen McKeown (13)	144
Abbi Taylor (13)	145
Beth Garrity (14)	146
Darren Lloyd (14)	147
Alex Lynch (14)	148
Beth O'Donnell (12)	149
Daniel Lecoko (13)	150
Jordan Allen	151
Nicole Hartley (12)	152
Cindie Williams (12)	153
Shannon Willoughby (12)	154

The Poems

I Have A Dream

I have a dream, a dream that will change the world,
bring peace to the world, no more wars, no more suicide,
just a world of wonder and peace.
The world will choose.

I have a dream, a dream that will bring
happiness, celebrations of love,
friendship of kindness and plants of beauty.
The mighty world of life.

I have a dream, a dream that will show a new world,
diseases of doom will perish by cures of God,
parents of cruelty will change to parents of love and care
and the animals of slaughter will be saved.

I have a dream that rotten things are normal,
but that will change, soon the world becomes
the world of life.
As long as I'm happy, I have . . . *a dream!*

Alex McEvoy (13)
Bebington High Sports College, Wirral

I Have A Dream

How do you get a dream?
A dream to save the world,
A dream for poverty to stop,
And to kick racism out of the world?

I wish I could have a dream,
Where all suicide, death and drugs end.

I have a dream,
But that's a dream,
We are the ones,
The ones that have to help,
But if we don't do anything,
Our dreams do not come true.

Oliver Diggory (13)
Bebington High Sports College, Wirral

I Have A Dream

I have a dream poverty will be over
I have a dream for kindness and laughter
I have a dream for all wars to be over
I have a dream for celebrations never-ending.

I have a dream for racism to stop
I have a dream for food and drink
I have a dream of starvation ending
I have a dream for trees and flowers all around us.

I have a dream for unfairness to end
I have a dream for families to come together
I have a dream for animal cruelty to end
I have a dream for dreams to be fulfilled.

I have a dream, do you?

Kerry Wintersgill (13)
Bebington High Sports College, Wirral

I Have A Dream

I have a dream, a dream that makes me laugh,
a dream that makes me smile at people,
then they smile back.
My dream makes me feel ten feet high.
My dream makes me feel like I am on top of the world.
My dream is the best dream,
it is magnificent, incredible, fantastic, awesome! I have a dream like
everyone else in the world,
but my dream is the greatest one of all.

Jade Swann (12)
Bebington High Sports College, Wirral

I Have A Dream . . .

I have a dream that I have lots of money
Where I can go on holiday, where it's nice and sunny
I'd have a private jet,
And fly around to where I want to get.

I'd buy my sister a horse
And then give her money to buy a silver Porsche.

For my mum and dad, a house I would buy
And watch their smiles light up the sky.

This is everyone's dream I agree
But would it ever happen to me?

But I think happiness is worth much more than this
With my family I live in millionaire bliss!

Alex Brown (12)
Bebington High Sports College, Wirral

I Have A Dream

I have a dream,
My dream
Is to be seen,
Seen in front of a live audience,
The band play, I sing,
And the strangest thing,
Is that I'm not nervous,
Because when I'm up there,
I feel so happy,
I have butterflies in my stomach.
I sing, sing out loud,
I feel like screaming the words,
Just so I'm heard,
I'm out of breath, I look around
The lights flash round and round.

I have a dream.

Alice Corden (12)
Bebington High Sports College, Wirral

I Have A Dream

I have a dream,
I see the world.
Everything's so small.
I see my old house, like a building block I used to love.
My old school.
I remember daydreaming about this dream.

> The sunset is so beautiful,
> I don't want to leave.
> I'm sure I'll never forget this,
> I'm so tired,
> I don't want to go to sleep,
> I don't want to, but I know I must.

As I wake up, I wonder where I am.
I see a beautiful waterfall,
Surrounded by thousands of palm trees.
There's no one here,
But I can hear girls giggling and screaming.
I don't know where I am,
I look down and see flippers going into the water.
Mermaids!
I've really seen mermaids.
This must be paradise.
I keep on floating,
Further and further away,
In the hot air balloon.
I don't know where I will end up.

Rebecca Withers (11)
Bebington High Sports College, Wirral

I Have A dream

I have a dream
To swim in the deepest ocean,
To fly over the highest mountain,
See the rarest animals,
Climb the biggest trees,
Jump higher than the clouds in the light blue sky,
Camp in the biggest wood,
With the dancing sunlight.
See the brightest stars which spell out this is a dream,
But in this Heaven-like dream I know it's going to end,
By the shaking of my mother, I find myself in the nightmare.
That is my life in this cruel world,
Gently I wave goodbye to the dream
And start the torture day.
That is my dream.

Nick Crawford (11)
Bebington High Sports College, Wirral

I Have A Dream

I have a dream that I cure people,
important people,
people who matter, not to you,
but to me.
People with cystic fibrosis,
it is an illness that
you are born with,
I want to cure their worries,
for they don't know when their
hearts will stop,
all that they know is, they won't
live a full life,
like me and you.
But these people are very special to me,
so that is why my dream
matters, not to you,
but to me.

Jordan Mearns (12)
Bebington High Sports College, Wirral

I Have A Dream

I have a dream for war to stop
I have a dream for poverty to end
I have a dream for starvation to finish
I have a dream for terrorism to disappear
I have a dream that England will win the World Cup
I have a dream that when we win the World Cup
Everyone will be partying into the street.

Matthew Browning (13)
Bebington High Sports College, Wirral

I Have A Dream

I have a dream,

Hoping for a better world
And for us to stop the wars
Viruses and starvation
Eager to help.

And stop these things.

Dreams can never stop
Racism can stop
Each person can start helping
Animal cruelty
Meeting hand in hand, let us be the help,
and make a stand.

Angela Kay (13)
Bebington High Sports College, Wirral

I Have A Dream . . .

I have a dream to own a giant swimming pool
with water temperature at cool.

It will have its own water slide that curls and whirls
with the sides really wide.

I have a dream to be a billionaire with lots of money that I will share.
I'll earn all the money, by being a businessman
and own all the businesses I can.

I have a dream for England to win the World Cup in Germany
and for me to lift the cup up.

I have a dream to fly the world's fastest plane across the world
and seas and do it again and again.

Daniel Pearse (12)
Bebington High Sports College, Wirral

I Have A Dream

I have a dream
that one day war will stop
and laughter and kindness will
spread all over the world.

I have a dream
that people will join together
to stop pollution,
to make a better environment.

I have a dream
that poverty and disease
will be banished.

I have a dream
that England will win the World Cup,
because everyone will celebrate together.

I have a dream
that all this
won't be a dream anymore.

Jenny Weaver (13)
Bebington High Sports College, Wirral

I Have A Dream

If I were a giant looking down upon Earth,
What would I want to see?
I could play with the children,
And people's heads, but no one can mess up a dream.

My dream would be so powerful,
And wished upon with thought,
I would paint a rainbow,
One that never ends,
I would thank the people that,
Have helped and cared for me,
I would thank the world at once
For letting me be happy.

I would run against the criminals
And let the innocent live,
Put an end to poverty and let the people eat.
If only this were real and not just in my head.

I have a dream to fix the world
It's fixed into my head,
I wish my dream came true,
But know all hope is dead.

Sophie Moreland (13)
Bebington High Sports College, Wirral

I Have A Dream

I have a dream
That I own a big car.
I have a dream
That it is a Jaguar.
Magnificent white
That shines so bright.
I have a dream
That I have a mansion,
Three storeys tall and three houses wide.
It has twenty rooms and
A safe filled with money.
I have bodyguards
With discipline and muscles.

Matthew Evans (13)
Bebington High Sports College, Wirral

I Have A Dream

I have a dream,
It may one day come true.
It's all the things I want to do,
To meet Blanche from Corrie.

That would be great,
Imagine having her as a mate.
I'd like to try on her glasses
And dance through the cobbled street.

A drink in the Rovers
And a pie at Roy's Rolls.
Oh, to chat with Rita and Norris too.
Me and Blanche to gossip all day through.

Rosie, Craig, Sophie too,
Hopefully my dream will come true,
To be an actress and star in The Street,
Then all my favourites I could meet!

Catherine Thomas (12)
Bebington High Sports College, Wirral

I Have A Dream

I have a dream
For the world to be fair,
Where people don't stop and stare.

I have a dream
To have no violence,
No drugs, weapons,
None of that childishness.

I have a dream
For the world to be happy,
Children having fun
And adults being zappy.

If all of my dreams
Would come true,
The world would be better
For me and for you.

Josh Dunroe (13)
Bebington High Sports College, Wirral

My Dream

My dream is for the world to be a better place,
Where it does not matter about your race,
Where around the world we can all stop worrying,
Because in my dream there will be no bullying.
Where we can feel comfortable all the time,
Because in my dream there will be no crime.
Where every person in the world will be truthful
And kind, good-natured, friendly and peaceful.
If all of my dreams could just come true,
The world would be better for me and you.

Daniel Turner (13)
Bebington High Sports College, Wirral

I Have A Dream!

I have a dream
To be a monster,
But not one very scary.

A star in the film
Alongside Jim Carey.

A farmer with a sack of corn
Crawling through the field.

A warrior in Rome
Shaded by his shield.

A monkey in the jungle
Swinging happily through the trees.

A bee-catcher
With . . . well,
With the bees.

Fill your head with
All there is.
Wouldn't it be fun?
Oooh, what a whizz!

Amy Palin-Tune (13)
Bebington High Sports College, Wirral

I Have A Dream

I have a dream that the whole world would shine,
I have a dream that the world was mine.
I have a dream that racism never came,
I have a dream that I would have fame.
I have a dream that poverty was no more,
I have a dream there was never a war.
I have a dream that the world would unite,
No need for hatred, no need to fight.
I have a dream that the heavens would open up above,
And surround the whole wide world with love.

Liam Singh (13)
Bebington High Sports College, Wirral

I Have A Dream

I have a dream of a perfect world,
Where poverty or pollution wasn't,
Where no countries were Third World,
And disease had been destroyed.

I have a dream of a perfect world,
Where laws didn't need to be enforced.
Where no one was burgled
And everyone had respect.

I have a dream of a perfect world
Where war was non-existent,
Where no one was rated first, second or third,
I have a dream of a perfect world.

Jamie Unsworth (13)
Bebington High Sports College, Wirral

I Have A Dream

I have a dream
That he can see
And be me
For just one day,
And see what I can't say.

I have a dream
That there will be no more words,
They won't hit me like daggers and swords,
For just one day,
See why he is, his wicked way.

I have a dream
That one day when I'm not here
And he is out drinking a bottle of beer,
That someone will ask him why?
Why he did it,
Why I'm not here,
Why I'm no longer happy and no longer near.

Rebecca Clarke (13)
Bebington High Sports College, Wirral

I Have A Dream

I have a dream, my dream is to be a professional hairstylist.
I'm sitting in my salon, wondering about my life,
Watching my trainee hairstylists work to their highest ability,
Seeing that the customers are happy with their styles.
Styling my mum's hair every night when I get home,
Wondering what the next fashionable hair colour will be,
Hoping to be able to open another salon.
I have a dream,
I want to be a professional hairstylist.

Hannah Beckley (12)
Bebington High Sports College, Wirral

I Have A Dream

I have a dream
To eat a big ice cream,
To be a great footballer
And play in the England team.

I want to be a fish,
But not to be on a dish.
I want to swim in the sea.
Most of all, I want to be free.

Sam Bradley (12)
Bebington High Sports College, Wirral

I Have A Dream

I have a dream
About the day I've had,
Whether it was good or bad.

I have a dream
About my mates,
And my most important dates.

I have a dream
I had a puppy,
It was black, white and fluffy.

Rachel Brett (13)
Bebington High Sports College, Wirral

I Have A Dream

I have a dream
To go to Florida.
It's a longer walk than
Just down the corridor.
I hop on a plane
And fly past Spain.
After nine hours' flight,
It's nearly midnight.

I'm finally here
After confronting my fear.
Tomorrow I'm going swimming,
The sea outside is shimmering.
I just can't wait
To feed them bait.
I'm going swimming with dolphins.

I wake up in the morning,
My alarm clock sets off a warning.

I jump on my boat
And start up the moat.
My boat is set free,
I set out to sea.
Sunshine and Star are their names,
I try to keep them very tame.
As I jump in, I begin to grin.
My dream's come true,
Tomorrow I fly back to Crewe.

Victoria Young (12)
Coppenhall High School, Crewe

Poem!

I have a dream
To change the world,
For black and white
To be the same.

I have a dream
To change the world,
Equal rights
For black and white.

I have a dream
To change the world.
I know it won't
Ever happen.

Charlotte Edwards (12)
Coppenhall High School, Crewe

I Have A Dream

I have a dream
To be normal.
I don't really have a dream,
I just want to be myself.

OK then, I'm lying,
I want to be a F1 racer,
Going down the track, flying,
A bit like Michael Schumacher!

The only problem is,
Michael Schumacher is German
And I'm not keen on Germany,
So I'll change it to Rubens Barrichello,
He's from Brazil.

So that's what I want to be.
Now go away and stop questioning me.

Josh Dawson (12)
Coppenhall High School, Crewe

My Dream

I have a dream to open
A rescue centre for cats,
To help the kittens and cats to live,
Helping kittens and cats to survive,
Otherwise they will die.
Their owners will buy another one
And abuse it again,
Then I will have to go and save it,
And then I will give it to the vets
To make it well and happy again.

Kadie Leeson (12)
Coppenhall High School, Crewe

I Have A Dream

I have a dream.
Think of the children with no water or food,
People with no clothes,
Walking around in the nude.
Imagine your next meal, a plate of dust.
All this can be stopped if we all work together.

Jake Kitchen (12)
Coppenhall High School, Crewe

My Dream!

I have a dream
That one day animals will be free
And they will not be targets,
They will be treated equally.

Testing must stop
On innocent creatures
That have done nothing wrong.
Why do you do it?

These animals live innocent lives
And do nothing to harm us unless provoked.
Animals should be free,
Away from experiments and harm.

Rose Holbrook (12)
Coppenhall High School, Crewe

My Dream

I have a dream
That species of animals
Will not be targets,
Will not be centre of attention
For the wrong reasons,
Will not be victims,
They will be free,
Away from harm and pain.
Testing must stop
On innocent animals.
It is wrong and cruel,
It is killing living things,
Which, if human is illegal,
Which should be the same
For living creatures.
And I will stand tall
Until my dream comes true,
And that is my dream.

Bethan Ingham (12)
Coppenhall High School, Crewe

I Have A Dream

I have a dream
To be famous and new,
I want to be a dancer
Performing for you.

Costumes of colour,
Music to suit,
Moving on stage,
We all look cute.

Break dance, street dance,
Hip-hop and jazz,
Slow moves, quick moves,
They all look fab.

The crowd goes wild
When we finish the dance.
We bow and walk off,
We're so happy to prance.

I have a dream
To be famous and new,
I want to be a dancer,
Performing for you.

Holly Ashley (12)
Coppenhall High School, Crewe

I Have A Dream

I have a dream to go to New York,
Unfortunately it's too far to walk.
Sitting on a plane,
All I can see outside is rain.
In my five-star hotel it's all going well.

I wake up in the morning
As my alarm clock sets off a warning.
In comes my designer,
Reaching for her eyeliner.
12 o'clock, time for lunch,
Eating my salad with a crunch.

At the fashion show
The lights begin to glow.
Walking down the runway five times,
At least I don't have to remember lines.
The seats are all full,
At least a model's life isn't dull.

Here I am in the latest trends,
Pink or purple, it just depends.
People clap as I walk by,
To look my best, I have to try.
My dream's come true -
Finally I'm a model.

Lorna Whiston (12)
Coppenhall High School, Crewe

My Dream Poem

I have a dream
To help all the abandoned and abused animals
When people have been mean to them.

Helping them get better
From their tragic past,
Hoping to gain their trust back.

I have a dream
To help all the abandoned and abused animals,
Hoping one day this dream will be seen . . .

Laura Maher (12)
Coppenhall High School, Crewe

I Have A Dream

I have a dream
More friends should be made.
To have less enemies, to have less war,
To have less fights, to have less arguments.
For more teamwork, for more freedom.

James Johnson (12)
Coppenhall High School, Crewe

My Dream

I have a dream,
The grass is green,
I'm gonna be a plumber
Through the winter and the summer!

I'm gonna be rich,
Not live in a ditch.
I'm gonna be a plumber
Through the winter and the summer!

With my best mate Josh,
We're gonna make a lot of dosh.
I'm gonna be a plumber
Through the winter and the summer!

I'll be driving in my Ferrari
Cos the kids wanna go on safari.
I'm gonna be a plumber
Through the winter and the summer!

Scott Powell   (12)
Coppenhall High School, Crewe

I Have A Dream!

I have a dream,
It cannot be seen,
One of my main thoughts
Is of all the battles fought
And how it causes poverty.
I have a dream,
It cannot be seen.

I have a dream,
It cannot be seen.
We can stop poverty
Without causing controversy,
In worse off, poorer countries.
I have a dream,
It cannot be seen.

I have a dream,
It cannot be seen,
Until unhappy faces
Bear a happy smile.
I have a dream,
It can now be seen!

Leanda Scragg (12)
Coppenhall High School, Crewe

Cancer

I have a dream
That cancer will be cured.
It's not fair on people,
We all need to be reassured.

I have a dream
That life one day
Will be free from medication
And people will have a say.

I have a dream
That families shouldn't cry.
If we all stand together,
Less and less people won't have to die.

I have a dream
And I'll stand up and say
Cancer shouldn't be a part of life,
I will totally get my way.

Victoria Hatton (12)
Coppenhall High School, Crewe

Dreaming

My great dream is
To be a footballer
And become very rich.
I would like the power
To be a hero.
I want loads of skills
And to have powerful shots,
Just like real footballers,
For example, Ronaldinho,
Gerrard and Henry.
I want to play for England and Liverpool.
I want to be known all around the world,
And score lots and lots of wonderful goals!
Also, my name is *Fozzy!*

Alex Forrester (12)
Coppenhall High School, Crewe

My Dream

I have a dream,
My dream is to travel the world,
To see everything that can be seen,
To visit every country.
Why do I have this dream?
I do because I think the world's such an exciting place
And there is so much to do and learn,
Like why is the sky so blue?
And can you remember when
You heard for the first time, the world revolves
And you didn't believe it?
That's my dream.

Hannah Dowdall (12)
Coppenhall High School, Crewe

I Have A Dream

I have a dream
About cats and dogs,
Happy mice
And poorly frogs.

Cheetahs are fast,
Snails are slow,
There's an animal to rescue,
Let's go, go, go!

Slugs are thick,
Cats are clever,
I hope that dogs
Will last forever.

I have a dream
About lots of creatures,
They will never look the same
Because of their features.

Rebecca Stanley (11)
Coppenhall High School, Crewe

Stables

I have a dream
To become a trainer
Of many horses.
They'll sleep in stables
With valuable labels,
Known to all of the world.
They'll win their race
At just the right pace
And won't slow down to lose.
They'll have lots of stamina
And plenty of speed
To bring in the money
That we will need.
To keep the dream alive,
We must win.
Maybe one day like . . . Mikky Quinn.

Josh Bloor (12)
Coppenhall High School, Crewe

The Dream

I have a dream that's all I hear . . .
I have a dream, these words just make me sneer!
The reason is this, I'll tell you once . . .
If I don't have a dream
I won't crash and burn like a nonce.

Dreams are like pots of gold . . .
You could be wonderful and bold,
But if this fairy tale goes wrong,
Humiliated you'll be for far too long.

So my advice to you is this,
Dispose of your dreams
As if they were mould.

Sam Carter (12)
Coppenhall High School, Crewe

I Have A Dream

I have a dream
To be a make-up artist.
Mascara, eyeliner and all kinds of cream,
To put on people while they dream.
Eyeliner to make their eyes look finer,
Creams to make their skin look smoother,
Mascara to make the boys move.

I have a dream
To make people look nice,
Beautiful, full of sugar and spice.
I get out my lipgloss
As I do up Kate Moss.
As I finish her face,
I start to pack my case.

Hillal Sleiman (12)
Coppenhall High School, Crewe

My Dream

I have a dream
Of being seen,
Caring for abandoned horses.
It all started when I was ten,
And now it's started all over again.
I saw a horse
Covered in cuts and sores,
With its head drooping down,
Right to the ground.
I want to show people why
You should let horses live, not die.
Some horses are in the news
Because they have been abused.
It made me know why
I want to help horses live, not die.
That's my dream.

Rachel Surridge (12)
Coppenhall High School, Crewe

My Dream

I have a dream . . .
To help all the unfortunate people in the world,
Save them from hunger, abuse and cruelty.
To help all the animals from abuse and cruelty
Such as killing them for no reason
And leaving them abandoned in the cold,
Letting them freeze to death.
I want to give them a life worth living,
They are innocent,
What have they done to deserve
The cruelty they get from people?
We need to save the world from horrible people,
Like poachers, butchers and loads more.

We need to save each other from horrible things,
Such as hunger, racism, abuse.
We need to give them a life worth living.
Stand up to racism,
Say no, or else you will regret it.

Katie Hughes (12)
Coppenhall High School, Crewe

I Have A Dream

I have a dream where
I can become famous and rich.

I have a dream that
The cruelty against animals would stop.

I have a dream where
I can go on 'Big Brother'.

I have a dream where
I can become thin and muscular.

Darren Burton (15)
Hill Top School, Gateshead

I Have A Dream

I have a dream
That Superman was real,
That Christopher Reeve was cured,
That everyone worked together for good
And the world was a safer place.

I have a dream
That all men are supermen,
That all women are superwomen,
That all children are superkids,
That there are no more wars.

I have a dream
That when natural disasters happen,
Super people are there to help,
That super doctors can cure the injured
And make people walk again.

I have a dream
That diseases are cured,
Accidents are prevented,
That justice is fair and swift,
That people learn from the past.

I have a dream.

Daniel Carr (15)
Hill Top School, Gateshead

I Have A Dream

I have a dream
That one day life will be
Like a Walt Disney film,
Where there's joy, fun and laughter
And happy ever after.

I have a dream
That good people lose but learn
The error of their ways
And become good themselves.

I have a dream
That hard work is rewarded,
That laziness is defeated,
That children play games fairly
And grow up loved and happy.

I have a dream.

Zoe Brown (15)
Hill Top School, Gateshead

Grandma

My gran was great,
She always inspired me,
She never said no,
Always helped me,
But now she's gone.
I still hear her voice
Telling me what to do,
Helping me with everything,
I still miss her.
Even though she's gone,
I still see her face,
But now she's gone
I miss her so.

Casey Gee (12)
Hindley Community High School, Wigan

Secret Inspirer

I have a secret inspirer.
Everywhere I look, he's waiting there for me.
He's out on the street with his mates every day.

He's very good at football, he plays every day.
He has scored two goals and he asked me to play.

Then he goes home on his bike and tells me goodbye.
This is why he inspires me.

Hannah Clark (12)
Hindley Community High School, Wigan

The Best

The morning,
The breakfast laid on the table,
Yes, she is the best.
She is caring, kind and understanding.
Yes, she is the best.
She makes your bed for you
When you come home from school.
Yes, she is the best.
Makes your tea at dinner time.
Yes, she is the best,
The best . . .
My mum.

Erin Garrett (12)
Hindley Community High School, Wigan

I Have A Dream

A girl one day said,
'I am sick of life.'
Her mother didn't take any notice,
Thought it was a phase.

Yet the mother didn't know
The girl was getting bullied.
She had made a hole that
She couldn't get out of!

Not going too far into detail,
It was boyfriend trouble.
You see, there was a big age gap,
A lot of people weren't happy.

In the mornings,
She wouldn't go out of the door.
A concerned friend came round every morning
And shoved her out of the door to school.

She would get dirty looks
From people across the yard.
People would yell all sorts of things,
But her friend told her to keep strong.

After this day, the girl went home
And no one heard from her for a while,
Until they all got invitations to her funeral.
Then it finally dawned on us.

It dawned on me when I was standing beside her grave.
How could I have let this happen?
I am to blame.
I am to blame.

My goal is to not spread
Any lies or rumours.
That girl would have had dreams,
Goals to reach, that I have ruined.

She never got there,
Yet I know,
I will!

Jodie-Lee Bushell (13)
Hindley Community High School, Wigan

She's The Girl!

She's the girl
Who everybody hates.
She's the girl
With hardly any mates.
She's the girl
Filled with regret.
She's the girl
Who everyone's met.
She's the girl
Hurting each day.
She's the girl
Who can't find her way.
She's the girl
Who is now dead.
She's the girl
Who meant what she said.
Because of this,
I'm the girl hurting each day,
Wondering why I couldn't help her find her way.
I'm going to be a better mate,
Thinking about love, not hate.
This girl made me realise
That there is more to life
Than spreading lies.

Rebecca Cusick (13)
Hindley Community High School, Wigan

England

When England stroll on the pitch,
I want to cheer them on.

When Robinson saves the ball,
I need the gloves he wore.

When Gerrard whips it in,
I carry the chant on.

When Terry stops the danger,
I give a sigh of relief.

When Cole weaves through the players,
I sit on the edge of my seat.

When Owen hammers it in,
I leap up and shout.

When England lifts the cup,
I am proud to wear my shirt.

Come on, England!

Curtis Baxter (13)
Hindley Community High School, Wigan

I Have A Dream

I have a dream, I wish I was in Heaven,
Living a life of pure luxury,
From hours nine 'til seven.
The Earth down below,
Far from the holy cloud
Where the pearly gates glow.

The angels shall be my friends,
With halos, wings and all,
With the happiness God sends,
Heaven's our home as we recall.
Never time to worry or fret
As each day goes quickly by,
But sometimes slow, I bet!

Ten good deeds every day
Is very tiring indeed,
But it's how the angels play
And it's good to succeed.
The light in my head will brightly gleam,
But this dream is just a dream.

Ami Green (12)
Hindley Community High School, Wigan

Dad

There has been so much hurt in my life, in the past.
There is always something making me alert
To the time that passes so fast.
Too many hearts have been burst,
Opened with such anger.

Frustration caused such pain,
Anxiety caused such sadness,
All this because of one hurtful man, *Dad*.

He's never in too fast,
He hurts his family and others all around,
He never listens to a thing we say.

Anger all around me, surprised at such a phase,
Nobody hears my screaming
As I'm hurt along the way.

I pray at night for this to stop,
But God doesn't hear my cries.

Dad hears my cries and howls, screaming for help.
He pounds me even harder 'til I fall upon the ground.
He walks away with no remorse, as if to say, 'not mine',
But deep inside I know he cares but just finds it really hard.

There's something deep inside my heart
Saying please forgive him.
I don't want him to know that I care too,
So I just dodge him all the time.

His mind plays tricks on him when he is alone,
Saying that he loves me,
Then he says he doesn't.

I feel I want to say, 'It will all be OK,'
But I want to prove him wrong of me,
To make him see that I can survive.
I can succeed, but he just doesn't believe in me.

Anna Varetto (13)
Hindley Community High School, Wigan

I Had A Dream

Through my life I've always had dreams,
Dreams of lifting the World Cup,
Bringing peace to our world,
Eradicating the wars that have been started,
But one thing I want, that is most important for me,
Is to live in harmony with the animals of Mother Earth.
They are dying out, becoming extinct.
It is because of us that they are dying out,
We have no excuse for any of this.
So come, my brothers, let us make peace
With these magnificent creatures
And cleanse this planet of all our sins,
For if this happens and that peace is restored,
May God forgive us for all that we did.

Philip Campbell (15)
Lord Lawson of Beamish School, Birtley

I Have A Dream

I see people taking drugs

H orrible things to take
A lot of these drugs can ruin your life
V ery, very bad
E very time you take them, your life is getting worse

A good thing to do is burn them

D estroy dangerous drugs!
R ight or wrong, it's easy to tell,
E very time you see a drug
A lways put it back
M any people have wasted their lives, stop this now!

Charlotte Middis (12)
Lord Lawson of Beamish School, Birtley

I Had A Dream

I had a dream
That I was eating ice cream
And I dropped the ice cream,
What does it mean?
Does it mean I am going to drop?
Does it mean I am going to die?
What, what does it mean?
I really don't know what it means,
All I know is
That this ice cream is melting
On my hand!

Lauren Fiddes (15)
Lord Lawson of Beamish School, Birtley

I Have A Dream

I have a dream that man and woman,
Boy and girl can live in a world of love.

No protesting, violence, racial hate and sex discrimination,
The people that initiate these petty little attacks,
Have they not got anything else better to do?
Are they really that shallow and dense?

Why? I don't understand why?
What is the point in being stereotyped?
Some people can be nice to you and then the next
Thing you know, they shoot you in the heart.

It's quite sad I think,
They'll hate you, they'll judge,
They'll treat you as a insignificant individual,
But you don't care because you're bigger than them.

If you walk away, you overcome these pointless remarks
It may make you feel tiny and worthless
But they're the worthless ones, not you.

However in a world of dreams,
A dream is only a dream.
We live a reality! Not a dream.

Steven Gardner (15)
Lord Lawson of Beamish School, Birtley

I Have A Dream

My dream is plain and simple,
Zero terrorism and zero nuclear weapons.
Why should we live in fear and anguish?
Why should we live in terror and pain?

Terrorism and weapons are more developed,
People's fear then grows.
Why can't they understand the heartache
That I will never know?

Kidnapping and public execution on video,
The fear of weapons grows.
Innocent people being killed,
Nobody knows why.

Simon Gray (15)
Lord Lawson of Beamish School, Birtley

I Have A Dream

I have a dream,
A dream of a perfect world.
A world without war, crime or hate.
A world full of peace, joy and success.
No anger, no rage; no shadow, no failure,
No hunger, no suffering, no contempt, no destruction,
No pollution, terrorists, abuse or drugs.
A world of serenity,
A world of purity.
I have a dream,
A dream of a happy place.
A place for a smiley face,
A place without fear or depression.
No anger, no rage; no sadness, no failure.
No stress, no worries; no tears, no terror.
No death, shadow, evil or pain.
A world of life,
A world of light.
I have a dream,
A dream of a perfect person,
A person without jealousy, obsession or greed.
A person bearing kindness, gifts and calm.
No desires, no darkness; no hate, no judgement.
No anger, no rage; no evil, corruption.
No weapons, power, advantage or prejudice.
A nice person,
A good person.
I have a dream.

Richard Nicholson (15)
Lord Lawson of Beamish School, Birtley

I Have A Dream

I have a dream.

H aving a dream is always something you want to achieve in life.

A nd whether it's to stop a crime, world hunger, terrorism, racism,
   illegal drugs, cruelty, or to have world peace or even to become
   a sports star, everyone has a dream.

V ery much,

E veryone wants a dream and wants to achieve it.

A lways stick to it and try to make it happen

D on't stop or it will stop and never come true

R egard all your dreams and they'll happen and you will be happy

E veryone will achieve something in life, whatever it is

A in't there anyone out there in the world who doesn't have a dream
   and want it to come true

M aybe 9 times out of 10 it will happen but just to make sure
   it happens, always remember to have a dream.

Shaun Stoneman (15)
Lord Lawson of Beamish School, Birtley

I Have A Dream

It's now time . . . the moment I've been waiting for my whole life,
Roars like lions ringing around me,
Cheers and boos as loud as anything that I've ever heard,
I'm looking around at anxious faces,
But now it is time . . .
I run for my life towards my destiny,
Only one will try and stop that,
So as I go forward, there's no going back
I close my eyes in belief, then . . .
Roars! The greatest uplift ever has finally come,
So I've climbed mountains and nearly fallen
But I reached for the stars and grabbed destiny,
Now that I conquered glory,
It's not enough for me as a local.
It is my dream to be . . .
The local hero.

Daniel Temple (15)
Lord Lawson of Beamish School, Birtley

I Have A Dream

I have a dream that all the terrorists in the world
Could find out what it's like for the victims' families and friends
The tears, the heartbreak and the anger
All the emotions they go through
And then terrorists might find out how bad it actually is
They all must not have a heart for doing it
I think we should do to them
What they have done or are planning to do to others
Make them and their families feel the pain.

Alexandra Trewick (14)
Lord Lawson of Beamish School, Birtley

I Have A Dream

I have a dream about terrorism!
I wish for a world without terrorism,
It's not fair innocent people die.
What they said was a lie,
There were no weapons of mass destruction,
There were no such things in production,
So in we sent our army force
To the front line they marched,
Searching for Saddam Hussain
In my eyes it's insane!

Soon after the fighting broke out
Men died and gave a shout
Guns start blazing, people started screaming
And debris was all over the floor,
It's a terrible thing, war.

Later that year, above in the air,
Hussain was found under the floor,
So we cheered, sang
And with a bang, it started all again
And it's truly insane.

Callum Anderson (13)
Lord Lawson of Beamish School, Birtley

I Have A Dream

I have a dream to have peace in our world

H ey, let's get rid of wars and crimes
A nd have our world normal again
V anish with heartbreakers and people that cause deaths
E veryone needs to learn about bad pain

A nd good pain

D on't let everyone tell you the world is a bad place
R eally it's not
E ven though everyone says it's so make your world
A peaceful place.
M ake our world a place where you would like to live.

Do you really want death and pain?

Iris Winley
Lord Lawson of Beamish School, Birtley

Imagine

Imagine
A world without bin Laden
There would be no Al Qu'aida and no London bombings.
Imagine
A world without Saddam
There would be no war and fighting in Iraq.
Imagine
A life without war
I think ITV news would be pretty poor.
Imagine
Iraqis and Brits singing a reunion song
But that wouldn't happen because they can't get along.
Imagine
If they don't stop fighting in Iraq
I'll give them a flipping, big smack.
Imagine
If war wasn't on the news every day
I would love it, it would be great.

I really wish there was no war
There's better things to think about and much, much more.

Imagine.

Craig Harrison (13)
Lord Lawson of Beamish School, Birtley

I Have A Dream

Imagine a world without terrorism
Imagine a world without war
Imagine men killing themselves
Imagine them on the floor.
We only have a certain time to live
Don't give it away.
There is no point in war.
So stop it once and for all
Don't let terrorists have their way.
This should not be a dream.
We should have it easy as cream.

Scott Fallon (13)
Lord Lawson of Beamish School, Birtley

Stop It Now

We are all different,
Not the same,
There's no need to be ashamed,

I hold a pen in my hand,
And make a list of my demands,
I raise my voice and shout out loud,
Hey you bullies, stop it now!

They find a fault,
No matter how small,
They think that they're
So big and tall.

Why can't people just be nice?
It's not really that hard,
Together we can make them stop,
So bullies listen up . . .

In my dream,
You're all extinct,
You never did exist,
So change your ways,
Or pack your bags,
My dream will come true!

Charlotte Hollins (13)
Lord Lawson of Beamish School, Birtley

I Have A Dream

I stand for something
I feel so strong
It's disgraceful and disgusting
And it makes you pong!

It affects a lot of things
Such as you and me
It adds to pollution
I would like to see . . .

All cigarettes thrown away
For people to stop
And start a new day
Don't they know it harms us
To cigarettes say, 'No!'

I stand for something
So I don't fall for anything
Help me stand for my dream
Help the world shine like a sunbeam.

Megan Kirton (13)
Lord Lawson of Beamish School, Birtley

Global Warming

I was thinking
About a world without penguins
People have electricity
But at the cost of all the ice
I was thinking
About a world without grass
People will burn everything
Then the human race will burn
In a world of global warming.
Stop it now!

Liam Scott (12)
Lord Lawson of Beamish School, Birtley

To Not Be A Nobody

I have a dream . . .

I want to be famous
To be a celebrity
To be a fashion model
And to be pretty.

I want to go on TV
Not to drop out of school
To be tall and thin
That would be totally cool.

To get good exam results
To have curly hair
To have a healthy diet
And for my hair to be fair.

To look young forever
Be cool for eternity.

Basically I want to be a celebrity
To be known all over the world
To go on national TV
And for my hair to be curled.

Tori Adams (12)
Lord Lawson of Beamish School, Birtley

I Have A Dream

I have a dream to achieve what I want in life
An education that will help me get through.

Don't you?

I have a dream to have lots of friends
To care for me and understand me
And just like me for who I am.
Even if I had only one good friend
Who does things for me
And they or my friend
Will get the same in return.

I have a dream to live a normal life
Then one day lead a life of my own
Get married and live with someone
And call my friends over the phone.

I have a dream to dream,
You know what I mean.

Natasha Brown (12)
Lord Lawson of Beamish School, Birtley

I Have A Dream

I have a dream, that could change the world

H orrible, the fact people are racist
A nd so what, he is black, I am white, it doesn't matter
V ery few people care if they hurt others' feelings.
E ffects everyone.

A nd it sickens and upsets me.

D ream, that's what I do!
R emember it's against the law to be racist
E veryone should try to put a stop to it
A nd I dream
M aybe someday I will succeed,
    maybe I will be that voice in the crowd.

Sophie Fletcher (12)
Lord Lawson of Beamish School, Birtley

No More!

I lay down and rest my head
Drifted off to another world
I'm there . . .
Clear air, fresh and free
Not a car in sight
Happy faces I can see.
No mobile phones,
To distract me.
I can't believe it
It has happened,
Global warming is over!
I woke up with a start
And . . . I had a dream!

Jordan Fleming (11)
Lord Lawson of Beamish School, Birtley

I Have A Dream

I have a dream. A

H orrible and disgusting drug.
A n injection in the arm and then you feel
V ery relaxed and rushy.
E xtremely, effectively harmful.

A nd then

D estroys people's lives
R ather kill yourself now
E xcellent it may seem, but
A n extremely addictive drug.
M akes people's lives a misery.

Sam Fyfe (12)
Lord Lawson of Beamish School, Birtley

I Have A Dream

I have a dream to go overseas,
I have a dream to do whatever I please,
I have a dream where the world is both black and white,
I have a dream that no one will fight,
I have a dream that everyone will be fed,
I have a dream that my poem will be read.

Sarah Howes (12)
Lord Lawson of Beamish School, Birtley

I Have A Dream

I have a dream which makes me think

H ow others must feel without a drink
A nd how people cope when they know they will die
V apour from the colours of others when they cry
E agerly awaiting for a sweet, kind voice

A nger bruises are not their choice

D anger hangs around any street
R apists are left to wander and defeat
E veryone is beautiful and unique
A nother one can be so weak
M y dreams can be so nasty, I'm glad it's not me.

Lauren Johnson (12)
Lord Lawson of Beamish School, Birtley

I Have A Dream

I have a dream
That there is no world hunger
My dream is food and water
If we had these delicacies
It would be great
Bricks and cement would give us a home
Old clothes of yours would keep us warm.

Doesn't matter if you're black or white
Fat or thin
Everybody is the same in this world
So why discriminate

Never take drugs like cannabis
Or any drugs at all
FRANK is there to help you
So if you're in need just call.

Matthew Kimmins (12)
Lord Lawson of Beamish School, Birtley

I Have A Dream

What is a dream?
Is it something you want to achieve?
Is it something you want to change?
Is it something you want to create?
Or . . .
Is it what you dream about at night?
A dream is anything,
From what you want to do tomorrow
To what you want to do in twenty years time
At night I dream about happiness
I dream about sadness
I dream about excitement
I dream about life . . .
What is a dream?
Is it something you want to achieve?
Is it something you want to change?
Is it something you want to create?
Or . . .
Is it something you want to dream about at night
A dream is anything!

Hannah Lancaster (12)
Lord Lawson of Beamish School, Birtley

I Have A Dream

I have a dream to ban all drugs

H ow do they take the things that gives bugs
A ll the time people are dying
V ery bad because they are buying
E arly morning they feel bad

A ll the more they think they're glad

D reaming, dreaming about the feel
R aging for drugs instead of a meal
E cstasy is one of them
A ll the addicts say it's a gem
M ayor, Prime Minister ban all drugs, even cigarettes.

Ben Skipsey (12)
Lord Lawson of Beamish School, Birtley

I Have A Dream

I have a dream,
That animals were heard and seen,
That people felt like this,
That my words can be bliss.

I have a dream,
That people were less mean,
That everything can speak,
Not bark, miaow and shriek.

I have a dream,
That every human being,
Would love a wag of a tail,
Not a pet's tragic tale.

I have a dream.

Zoë Timney (12)
Lord Lawson of Beamish School, Birtley

I Have A Dream

Football
World peace
No crime
No pollution
No litter
World hunger
Schools

My dream is for people to talk about things instead of having wars
And for people to stop committing crimes.
Also I don't want people polluting the air with car fumes.

Lee Walker (12)
Lord Lawson of Beamish School, Birtley

I Have A Dream

I have a dream that I will never get a detention in school
And will always be on my best behaviour and will never talk.

I have a dream that in my GCSEs I will get very high marks
And then will move into 6th form.

I have a dream that one day I will be a super star
And will sing 'No Promises' with Shayne Ward.

I have a dream that when I am older I will be a paramedic
And will save lots of people's lives.

I have a dream that I will be in a film
And I will be one of the main characters.

I have a dream that I will have a famous husband
Who I will spend the rest of my life with.

I have a dream that I will live in a huge mansion
With my husband and four children.

I have a dream that in my mansion I will have 3 dogs,
5 puppies, 3 kittens and 2 fish.

I have a dream that I will never ever get ill
With anything and will live till I am older than 100.

I have a dream that when I die I will have a very expensive funeral
And will be buried in a pink coffin.

Sarah Cooper (11)
Lord Lawson of Beamish School, Birtley

I Have A Dream

I have a dream that things will calm down,
I have a dream that wars will stop,
I have a dream that terrorism will stop,
I have a dream that hunting will stop.

I have a dream that slavery will stop,
I have a dream that new laws be made,
I have a dream that murders will stop,
I have a dream that my hopes come true.

Michael Fella (12)
Lord Lawson of Beamish School, Birtley

I Have A Dream

I have a dream,
To be a footballer.
I was rich with a big house,
And I had a pet mouse.
I played for Real Madrid
Then I had to get rid,
So I came back home
And got myself a loan,
So then I played for Sunderland
And got them promoted.
Then I bought a house
And got my mouse,
Scored loads of goals,
Celebrated them with loads of rolls,
Then I woke up.

Adam Fisher (12)
Lord Lawson of Beamish School, Birtley

I Have A Dream

I have a dream to be a soldier
To fight for a right
For discipline and honour

To fly in the RAF
To find my imaginary friend, Jeff

To be a star like Beckham
To play on my game called 'Tekken'.

Niall Monehen (12)
Lord Lawson of Beamish School, Birtley

I Have A Dream

I have a dream,
Or so it may seem,
I have a dream inside my head,
Then I wake up inside my bed,
I know it might not be real,
But my dream was to ride on the big wheel.

I have a dream,
Or so it may seem,
Swimming with dolphins in the sea,
Hope it's not too cold for them and me,
To get a suntan on the beach,
Not to be nibbled on the toes by a leech.

I have a dream,
A wonderful dream,
Everyone wants a dream,
Everyone needs a dream,
My dream is what I want,
My dream is what I need,
I have a dream,
Or so it may seem.

Samantha Parmenter (12)
Lord Lawson of Beamish School, Birtley

I Have A Dream

I have a dream,
That no one will scream.
At violence in the street
And people will bow at another's feet.
I see today,
That people need to pay.
For what they have done,
At the point of a gun,
Loved ones die,
While others cry.
I see innocents in jail,
Getting cold, off the hail.
I see crimes,
In our times.
I don't want to,
But I have to.

Michael Rear (11)
Lord Lawson of Beamish School, Birtley

I Have A Dream

I have a dream just one dream
To be the next Ronaldinho,
I don't want to be the best,
I want to be the very best,
I won't stand for second best,
Only the very best!

I have a dream, just one dream,
To be the next Michael Schumacher.

I don't want to be the best,
I only stand for the very best
I don't stand for gold
I only stand for platinum.

I have a dream, just one dream
To be the next Barry Sheen
He is the best, the very best
And only the best
That's what I'm going to be

I have a dream, just one dream
To be the next Eddie Kid
The best better than all the rest
Better than Evil Knievel.

Joe Storey (12)
Lord Lawson of Beamish School, Birtley

I Have A Dream

I have a dream, that I will have fame
I would play for Newcastle, well any team
Apart from Sunderland of course,
I hate them the most.
Newcastle have skilful players
From all different countries
Emre, Luque and many, many others.

I have a dream that I will be like Shearer
Who can drill a ball, like a bullet from a gun,
Every player has a role to play,
Like Owen who bangs goals in every day.

But my biggest dream of all time,
Is to make world peace,
I would stand out, in front of a massive crowd,
And say what I shall say,
Less crime and more good times,
It is terrible in Iraq, Afghanistan too,
So make world peace and we will be safe, me and you.

James O'Boyle (12)
Lord Lawson of Beamish School, Birtley

My Dreams

My dreams are fighting in wars
Or I'm a spaceman heading for Mars
Sometimes I'm flying through the air
Maybe I'm wrestling with a wolf or a bear
But the dream that I like the best and the most
Is when I saw my nana as a ghost

Sometimes I'm frightened of scary things
Or I'm playing basketball with real human beings
Once I dreamt I was breathing underwater
And to be king and have a new world order

Last night I dreamt I'm racing a car
And to be an actor or a superstar
But when I did see my nana as a ghost
It truly was the one I liked the most.

Adam Burns (12)
Lord Lawson of Beamish School, Birtley

I Have A Dream

I have a dream of being famous
Either a swimmer, footballer or athlete,
Or a world record breaker, to survive boiling heat.
I would like to make the world a better place
And I would want to enter a marathon race.
I would like to stop terrorism
And create heroism.
In my dream, I would like to be known across the world
I would like to stop racism
I would like to join Newcastle
And stop all of the hassle.

I have a dream of all sorts of things
And sign up with football teams like Real Madrid and Arsenal.
I want to be on TV
And stop battles of nations, as work from me.
I want to stop all war,
And give the people more.

Liam Kelly (12)
Lord Lawson of Beamish School, Birtley

I Have A Dream

My dream is to be a fashion designer
And own shops all around the world
Like Paris, London, Milan and New York.
I want to be very wealthy
I've always been interested in fashion,
Shopping and style.
I want to design the nicest clothes,
Shoes and accessories.

Rachel Bills (12)
Lord Lawson of Beamish School, Birtley

I Have A Dream

I have a dream, that one day,
I will have a stunning horse,
I will ride carefully around a course,
My horse will be black,
It will have expensive, shiny tack,
I will own my own yard and other people
Can keep their horses there,
I will give my horse lots of love and care,
So this is how my life will be
A lovely life just for me!

Sophie Muncaster (11)
Lord Lawson of Beamish School, Birtley

I Have A Dream

I have a dream that I could fly.
I have a dream that I was from the ghetto.
I have a dream that I was Superman.
I have a dream to eat alphabet spaghetti.
I have a dream that I was a Polo.
I have a dream that I was a turkey.
I have a dream that I was the Queen.
I have a dream that I was a banker and I bank all day.
I have a dream to be Shakira.
I have a dream to be a pretzel.
I have a dream to be Jakie Q not Jackie P.
I have a dream to eat a lemon.
I have a dream to be the child catcher.

Jordan Hutchinson (12)
Lord Lawson of Beamish School, Birtley

I Have A Dream

I had a dream about a world with no school,
That I have a mansion with a great big pool.
I had a dream that I was allowed a dog,
Cats, rabbits, guinea pigs, even a frog.
I had a dream the world was made of candy,
The beach was made of sherbet, it looks all pink and sandy.
I had a dream that I could fly,
I could see all the world from in the sky.
I had a dream I became a star,
I could bring world peace, there wouldn't be another war.
I had a dream that no one picked on me,
That I could run away from the bad things, I'd be happy and free.
I had a dream everyone I hate would disappear,
That would be good, I wouldn't have to fear.
I had a dream that all the stars fell down,
I gathered them up to make a sparkling crown.
I had a dream we went on an adventure,
We found the X and found loads of treasure.
I had a dream I was never ill, always healthy,
That I was happy, famous and also quite wealthy.
I had a dream I could have anything at all,
All the best things like my own graffiti wall.
I had a dream that I went on a shopping spree,
Everything I wanted I got bought for me.
I had a dream that this poem would now end,
Oh wait that was real, so I don't have to pretend.

Joanne Simm (12)
Lord Lawson of Beamish School, Birtley

I Have A Dream

I have a dream
With a world made of chocolate.
I have a dream
That there was no school.
I have a dream
That I had a big outside pool.
I have a dream
That I was so rich.
I have a dream
That I could meet a witch.
I have a dream
That my kitten never ran away.
I have a dream
That it was the last school day.
I have a dream
That it was Christmas Day.
I have a dream
That it was my mum's pay day.
I have a dream
That I could fly.
I have a dream
That my baby cousin wouldn't cry.
I have a dream
That my neighbours weren't loud.
I have a dream
That I make my parents proud.
I have a dream
That I cannot tell.
I have a dream
That I had a magic wishing well!

Rebecca Telford (11)
Lord Lawson of Beamish School, Birtley

I Had A Dream

I had a dream on that it seemed.
It was on the 18th May,
That's when I had to play
At Newcastle stadium.

Taking over Shearer,
Who was a great player.
I was the kind of player
Who was being talked about
Saying it shows you're the
The best from the rest.
Is this going to be my success?

Running onto the pitch
For the very first time.
Tick-tock, it's half-time
1-0 down, I had 45 minutes
To turn it around,
80 minutes in the game,
At stand still at 1-1
With all the supporters
Looking like clowns
91 minute, we have a free kick
It's in, 2-1 to Newcastle
The UEFA Cup Final.

Michael Winley
Lord Lawson of Beamish School, Birtley

I Have A Dream

I have a dream
To play for the team
England
That's my dream.

A winning goal for me to score
In the World Cup against Equador
For my name to be known
By footy stars like Martin Keown

Then to sign for The Toon
And score against those United goons
Wipe that smile of their faces
And relegate Sunderland who are a disgrace.

Tom Bowe (12)
Lord Lawson of Beamish School, Birtley

I Have A Dream . . .

I have a dream, that one day there will be no wars,
The world will be peaceful
And people won't have to do chores.

I have a dream, that all murderers would be locked up,
There would be no killing of animals
Like tiny, tiny pups.

I have a dream, that one day African orphans will find hope
And helpless people in the world
Will find out how to cope.

I have a dream, that one day, people will not fight,
They will come and sing songs
All through the night.

I have a dream, that the world could be a better place,
Nothing bad would happen
And everyone won a race.

I have a dream, that one day doctors could find a cure for cancer,
And all of the victims of it
Could have a job as a dancer.

I have a dream, that one day someone will find this poem
And they will think of changing this world,
Just like I have today,
They will try so hard to make this world a better place.

I have a dream that the person that finds this poem
Will want all of these nice things to happen too.
They will make this world really nice, good and new.

Alexander Robson (12)
Lord Lawson of Beamish School, Birtley

I Have A Dream

D reams of being a pro runner,
   but everyone knows she's so much funnier.
R ampaging damage, Donya's coming,
   we all know she'll be a-running.
E ngland to win the World Cup,
   we all know they need to toughen up.
A rsenal win the Premiership,
   but soon we know they'll all just trip.
M ichael Owen out for a year,
   we all know it's a bit of a dare.

Kayleigh Lumsden (11)
Lord Lawson of Beamish School, Birtley

The Dreams Of A Teen's Angst

I have a dream
that you could fall in love and not get hurt
I have a dream
where you can have friends and not get betrayed
I have a dream
where you can be yourself and not get put down
I have a dream
that you can come home and not wish you were somewhere else
I have a dream
where girls don't believe suicide's the only way out
I have a dream
that girls don't believe they have to diet for a boyfriend
I have a dream
that you can have a normal life without something bad happening
I have a dream
where whenever you needed anyone,
I am there for you
I have a dream
that our life was perfect.

Stacey Davidson (13)
Lord Lawson of Beamish School, Birtley

I Have A Dream

A peaceful world
no hate, no fear,
I really hope
that time is near.

A place where war
is just unknown,
families together,
no one alone.

Where kindness shines
through everyone,
where no one's lost,
where no one's won.

Where no one's judged
for who they are,
where people's dreams
are never far.

A place where people
work as a team,
the sad thing is
it's just a dream . . .

Magda Nyadu (13)
Lord Lawson of Beamish School, Birtley

I Have A Dream

As I fell asleep, I started to dream
I dreamt of strawberries and ice cream.
I dreamt of flying through the stars
Oh my gosh, I was hitting Mars.
The clouds they tasted of candyfloss
Fluffy, nice and silky soft.
All my worries were swept away,
This dream will come true maybe today.

Rachael Ryles (14)
Lord Lawson of Beamish School, Birtley

I Have A Dream

Aeroplanes crash and tsunamis roar,
These things are happening more and more.
If they don't stop, there will be grief,
So I'll try and make my point quite brief.

I want things to stop; it's just not right!
It shouldn't really matter whether you're black or white.
People shouldn't care if you're overweight,
It's just no excuse to start picking on mates.

Crime is bad; it's more than wrong,
Rape and murder, gone on too long.
Crime and animal abuse is unjust,
It must be stamped out; that is a must.

Natural disasters and pollution in the air,
Mother Nature won't stop; it's just not fair.
I have a dream that these things stop,
Where the giving of kindness comes out on top.

Emma Eckford (13)
Lord Lawson of Beamish School, Birtley

I Have A Dream . . .

That I could walk alone at night,
Without being caught up in a fight.
That police didn't have to patrol around,
To listen out for the gunshot sound.
That the youth weren't supplying drugs,
And selling them to no good thugs.
That people didn't have to commit suicide,
To escape from their dreadful lives.
That one single person couldn't break your heart,
A pain that cuts like a thrown dart.
That the media didn't supply a message,
That makes young girls turn anorexic.
That prisons didn't have to stand,
So we could walk in a 'death free' land.
That everyone could be themselves,
And weren't branded like toys on shelves.
That someday my dream can come true,
Then the world can be anew!

I have a dream . . .

Hannah Cannon (13)
Lord Lawson of Beamish School, Birtley

I Have A Dream

I have a dream

H ave a world that's not racist
A nd not a world of anger
V irtue to stop world hunger
E nable world peace.

A nd watch Newcastle win the cup

D angers around the world end
R onaldinho coming to NUFC to
E nd Newcastle's cup problems
A red card and goal and win against
M anchester United and lead
    to Champions League fame.

That's my dream!

James Whitaker (12)
Lord Lawson of Beamish School, Birtley

I Have A Dream - You Are In It

I have a dream . . .
That life was not so cautious,
That we could be free and be whoever we wished.
I have a dream . . .
That I could fly and have power,
That I could change all evil to good.
I have a dream . . .
That I could be an achiever and have no one stop me in my path,
That success is only little and anyone could reach it.
I have a dream . . .
That someday, somehow, poverty will become a thing of the past,
That war and conflict is only a dream, not real at all.
I have a dream . . .
That she who thinks she is ugly and he who wishes he were white,
Could have freedom and the confidence they need.
I have a dream . . .
That life was not so cautious,
That we could be free and be whoever we wished . . .

Rebecca Oldham (13)
Lord Lawson of Beamish School, Birtley

I Have A Dream

I have a dream that blacks
And whites lived in peace and harmony,
Sharing sweets and setting places,
Not taking drugs and being racist.
I have a dream that animal cruelty
Will not take place in this world,
Kicking dogs and cats.
Leaving pets in dark, cold places, *brrr*.
This is my dream.

Jake Scott (12)
Park High School, Birkenhead

I Have A Dream

I have a dream, a dream of no cigarettes
And no smoke from them.
I hate cigarettes
Like I hate alcohol.
If we had no cigarettes or alcohol
There would be less people dying of cancer,
The dreaded cancer that kills people every day.
Cancer must be stopped, it kills around 100 people every day.
If we stop cancer people will stop losing family.
Then when we stop cancer we can live as one,
No one killing other people,
No hitting or skitting at other people.
If that happened there might not be any war,
No one being killed every three seconds.
Smoking also kills people who don't smoke,
Everybody knows it!

Kurtis Sinnett (13)
Park High School, Birkenhead

I Have A Dream

I have a dream,
A dream of where war is no more,
Of a place where pain is gone,
Of a place where everyone can live together peacefully,
Of a place where everyone can live as one,
Of a place where there is no more hunger,
No more thirst
And no more death.

I have a dream
Of a place where weapons are not used or needed,
Of a place where there is no more bullying,
Of a place with no one to pick on one another,
Of a place where everyone is different,
But there is no disagreement,
Of a place where everyone gets on,
Of a place where fights are never fought
And where no one needs to protect themselves.

I have a dream,
A dream of a perfect world.

Graham Stringfellow (13)
Park High School, Birkenhead

I Have A Dream

The world is mean it may seem,
But I have a dream
Where cruelty dies,
It starts with screams and cries,
Yells and shouts,
Pounds and pouts,
But not anymore,
Crime won't be there when I open my door,
No more screams and people dying,
Definitely no more crying,
No yells nor shouts,
No pounds or pouts,
It all ends here,
No more fear,
No sins,
No woes,
Just a garden where courtesy and loyalty grows.
Dream this dream with me and make it be!

Grace Dodd (12)
Park High School, Birkenhead

I Have A Dream

I have a dream that no more threats shall be said,
No more bullies shall threaten the innocent.
We will all live in peace, in harmony,
That's the way I would like it to be.

I have a dream that society will be a better place,
That the murderers will cease to take human lives.
The burglars will think twice before ruining a life,
That jail cells will become a thing of the past.

I have a dream that no child should ever
Know what it feels like to be hungry or alone.
That no child will be deprived of their parents love
And no child shall be beaten for any apparent reason.

I have a dream that police shouldn't be injured
For protecting the public. That soldiers shouldn't
Have to go to war to protect their country.
That no firemen should jeopardise their lives through
Someone else's carelessness.

I have a dream that these dreams come true,
If only to make the world a better place!

Aaron Dodd (12)
Park High School, Birkenhead

I Have A Dream

I have a dream that when I go to sleep
I will not hear a gunshot.
I have a dream that I will not hear someone
being beaten to death.
I have a dream that everyone in the world
has given up fighting.
I wish there is no more world hunger
and everywhere will be tidied.
I wish that all illness can be cured
and no one will die.
I wish that we do not depend on wealth all the time.
I have a dream that there are no more drugs.

Abigail Evans (12)
Park High School, Birkenhead

I Have A Dream

I have a dream . . .
Where everyone could walk,
Talk and feel whatever they choose.

They would never get hurt, never get bruised,
Never get blamed,
Always have the right to stand up
And fight for what they believe!
No matter what other people say.

If this dream was to come true then Earth
Would be like Heaven too.

Steven Gateley (12)
Park High School, Birkenhead

I Had A Dream

I had a dream that when I woke up there was no wars,
No fighting and football hooligans.
If countries got on it would be a happier world.
The world could be a better place if there were no wars and terrorists.
Why do they want to take their lives and lives of innocent people?
If the world didn't have wars
Most of the countries would be best mates instead of enemies!
And people should respect
Other people from different countries,
And not judge them by their colour.
There should be no such thing as racism
And then people would respect each other.
Why do football fans fight at the match?
They will just wreck what should be the beautiful game!

Tyler Neill (13)
Park High School, Birkenhead

I Have A Dream . . .

I have a dream to change the world,
To kick out all the bad,
To make the world a happy place,
So no one will be sad.

I have a dream for the world to change,
To get rid of all the crime,
To stop the drugs, bullies and bombers
And even stop the wars.

It shouldn't have to be this way,
With horrible people and abuse.
I have a dream to change the world,
For this there is no excuse.

It makes me angry when I hear the news,
About thieves and terrorists,
I want to stop all these horrible people,
They will never ever be missed.

Katrina Bimpson (13)
Park High School, Birkenhead

I Have A Dream

Violence and crime,
This is reality
All the time.

Poverty and ill health,
Against a background
Of white wealth.

Equality and what is right
Is worth
The fight!

I have a dream
Where life is not
What it seems.

Life without fear,
Laughter not crying
Is what I hear.

Freedom of speech
Is a goal
We can reach.

All fighting can cease,
Black and white
Can live in peace.
This is my dream!

Hannah Shaw (12)
Park High School, Birkenhead

I Have A Dream

I have a dream racism will no longer be,
For all the world to see.
Why do people do it?
People should just be able to go and sit,
Without anyone shouting nasty things.
I have a dream that black people can walk down the street
Without things being thrown or nasty comments said.
It is bad.
It is sad.
I have a dream children can go out playing
Without anyone name-calling or anyone to be saying
Any words that are unacceptable!
I have a dream that adults will walk down the street
Without being racist to each other.
We are all made the same.
Racism is lame.
Black and white people are not different from each other.
I have a dream that black people will have an easy life,
Not a hard life.
Black people should get treated the same as white people
Not a nasty way.
They aren't any different.

Nicole Carty (13)
Park High School, Birkenhead

I Have A Dream!

I have a dream
That racist people are gone,
Children out playing,
Nobody name-calling, nobody to be saying
Any words that are unacceptable!

I had a dream
That black people would live a happy life,
Not a hard, horrible, nasty life,
Without racist people surrounding them!

If this dream comes true
I'll be happy and joyful,
For the rest of my life,
Visiting places where I haven't been before!

Rachel Bardullas (13)
Park High School, Birkenhead

I Have A Dream

I had a dream that child abuse is bad,
All the kids that get it are really sad.
I had a dream of a girl called Grace,
She had cuts and bruises all over her poor little face.
As time goes by kids are getting abused,
Sometimes the people closest are the ones that get accused.
Cuts and bruises sometimes go away,
When the pain inside will always stay.
Now Grace is older and getting on with her life,
She is now helping others who are in trouble and strife!

Camille Brougham (13)
Park High School, Birkenhead

Smoking Kills

I have a dream that one morning
When I get up there is no smoking!
People smoke for kicks 'n' thrills,
But in the end it always kills.
My lungs are black and full of smear,
If I stopped my lungs would be clear.
When you inhale smoke it is no joke,
To live or die, to laugh or cry,
It's up to you what you do.
Smoking kills, it's plain to see,
Smoke if you wish, but don't kill me!
When people smoke it makes me cry,
It's worse for them because they may die.
Smokers cough, wheeze and stink,
Smoking should be banned I think!
Now it's time for me to go to bed,
In the morning another smoker is dead!
Which makes me feel lucky to be alive.
But in the end it's their own fault,
They shouldn't have smoked, they had the choice,
But now they have ruined their teeth and voice!

Sarah Guntrip (13)
Park High School, Birkenhead

I Have A Dream

Racism is everywhere
So please take care!
It's in football
And even in the hall!
They all get upset,
But they never get a threat,
Being racist is a crime,
If you are racist you will do the time!

Racism is everywhere,
Don't even do it for a dare.
We are all made the same,
So don't feel ashamed!
But whatever colour or creed you are,
In life we will go far
But we are all made the same!

Chris James-Parr (13)
Park High School, Birkenhead

I Have A Dream

I have a dream that racism will be kicked out.
Everywhere I go I get people telling me to go back to my own country.
That's what upsets me most,
It hurts people's feelings and thoughts as well.

I had a dream that black people could work
And not be terrorised.
To be able to walk down the street
And not have insults thrown at me.

If this dream comes true I will walk down the street
With my head in the air
And a white girl on my arm
And people will see me for who I am.

I had a dream I had two children,
A little black boy and a little black girl.
They played together with the little white kids in the street,
They skipped and played football and no one breathed a word.

I had these dreams when I was 13 years old.
I am now 34 and all of my dreams have come true.

Jessica Ferguson (13)
Park High School, Birkenhead

I Had A Dream

I had a dream that when I woke
All wars would be over.
All nations will join together and be as one,
No hatred, no wars, no heartache!
All will be replaced with laughter, happiness and smiles.
Maybe one day my dreams may come true,
And everything will turn out right.
Just peace,
Smiles in the wind,
Tears of joy!
All the nice things that come together.
Especially when I have my dreams to turn to.
When I had a dream.

Jamie Francis (14)
Park High School, Birkenhead

I Have A Dream

I have a dream
That we can live in society without jeopardy or hate,
I have a dream
That we can have a neighbourhood with love and care,
I have a dream
That the world will stop the hurt and just be nice,
All people are the same,
I have a dream
That hatred will be stopped in its path
And turned around back to where it came from,
I have a dream
That everyone gets on and nobody kills anybody
And nobody hurts anybody,
I have a dream
That everyone will be happy and loved,
That is my dream,
But that is just one dream,
If we all dream the same dream maybe it will become a . . .
Reality.
I have a dream, so should you!

Nathan Standing (13)
Park High School, Birkenhead

I Had A Dream

I had a dream I was black.
What's the difference, black or white?
Why do they always have to fight?
Black's black and white's white.
What's the difference? They're both alright.
Why do adults abuse young children?
Why do they beat them and try to kill them?
Why do they do that, it's not fair!
Don't their parents really care?
Why do people take drugs?
They're all just hooligans and thugs!
They just don't know the damage it can do,
If you get addicted, it could kill you!

Becky Taylor (13)
Park High School, Birkenhead

I Have A Dream

I have a dream that the world can be clean of drink and drugs.
Think of them as insects and bugs.
What's the point in them?
Making people crazy, then making them lazy!
Making people drowsy, then making them lousy!
When a woman hits the bottle
It's a life hitting the bottom.
When a man hits the drugs it's a life hitting the wall
And when a child hits the drink and drugs
Out come the insects and bugs
To make them crazy, then make them lazy.
Stamp out insects and bugs.
Stand up to drink and drugs.

Hollie Rugen (13)
Park High School, Birkenhead

I Have A Dream!

I have a dream to stop war,
Stop the war, it kills people!
You don't see your family in the week.
You don't have to fight different countries.
Countries don't have to fight.
Stop the war,
Then all the countries can be friends.
Could the war ever stop?
Please let it stop.
Life could be different without hearing on the TV
About people dying,
It's sad when you get told that a member of your family is dead.
The grief, the sorrow,
War should have never started.
Please stop the war!

John Bilton (13)
Park High School, Birkenhead

I Have A Dream

I have a dream that racism will stop,
That addiction to drugs can be forgot.
I have a dream those children stop getting beaten,
It's not nice to get that kind of greeting.
I have a dream that war will stop
And everyone can get on, no matter what.
I have a dream that killing and raping can stop
And always be forgot!
I also have a dream that everyone appreciates each other
And gets on, no matter what.

Kayleigh Brabander (13)
Park High School, Birkenhead

I Have A Dream

I have a dream of a much cleaner world,
A world where we can all join and link hands like hippies and sing,
Sing a song of praise and we can all get along,
And every time I see a flood I will always hope it turns out good,
With no death, injury or misery not long.
I have a dream of no crime in the world, no murder of a 'gangsta'
hood,
No violence or drugs or theft;
No piracy, not any left.

I have a dream of no bullying,
And everyone as friends, there'll be all laughs and no cries,
What's the point in the useless thing?
No one gets hurt, no one gets told off so now little kids can wipe
their eyes.

I have a dream of no drugs,
No cigarettes or booze, no drugs except medicines that's the
way it goes.
Drugs are little thugs,
What is the need in them? They don't cure your nose.
They make you act so crazy,
You could go into a trance,
You would kill at first glance, so burn, all drugs should burn
And get off the planet.

Ben Redfern (13)
Park High School, Birkenhead

I Have A Dream

I have a dream
That the world will come to peace.
Destroy all guns
And blow up all bombs.
Stop pollution
And global warming.
Forget about racism
And be kind to foreign people.
Get rid of terrorists
And it will stop the bombing.
Destroy animal cruelty
And keep more species alive.
Stop making drugs
And stop some deaths.
Kill bullying
And it could stop suicide.
Look after our environment
And it might stop natural disasters.
Stop crime
And we won't need any police.
Start working
And we will have low tax.
Ban execution,
Stop killing off our species.
Get rid of some alcohol
And stop drink drivers.
Stop poverty,
Give some money.
This is my dream
And I hope it comes true.

Jonathan Williams (13)
Park High School, Birkenhead

I Have A Dream

Lots of hurt, too much pain, so many cries,
So I hold my breath and shut my eyes.
I have a dream, the sky is clear,
Children laughing, there's no more fear.
The flowers are blooming and the grass is green,
The most beautiful sight I have ever seen.
I can see no more children, alone and afraid,
No more wars because peace has been made.
Laughter and shouts of joy fade away,
I guess in this world I'm not meant to stay.

The sound of screams flood my ears,
I shudder at the return of my fears.
I open my eyes and all I can see
Is violence and tears, no one is free.
People in poverty, people covered in dirt,
People throwing punches and always getting hurt.
When you see a stranger, why not give a smile?
Just do a little job, every once in a while.
So let's all unite in peace and harmony,
That is the world I would like to see.

Emma Williams (13)
Park High School, Birkenhead

I Have A Dream . . .

I have a dream . . .
To go outside and be happy.
Racism is a thing that should stop.
People can't control who they are,
Male are male, female are female.
We all share one world.
It doesn't matter if you're black or white,
The only thing that matters is how you are inside.
Racism is sometimes to do with the past,
Things that have happened in the past can never be changed.
Wars that have happened are in the past,
Why mention the past when it can hurt people's feelings?
Words do hurt,
Mentioning things in the past does hurt people.
It doesn't matter what we are,
The only thing that matters is who we are.
We live our life to the death,
Why waste our life on ruining others?
Life is too short to hurt people.
So let's work together and stop!
Full stop!

Andy McNally
Park High School, Birkenhead

I Have A Dream . . .

I have a dream of absolute peace,
A world with no war or crime increase.
I dream of a world where everyone loves,
Where nobody fights, hits or shoves.
I hope if we all show true heroism,
We can once and for all, wipe out terrorism.
Everyone will learn from their mistakes,
Where everyone shares, not just takes.

I dream no man, woman or child lives in fear,
Where no one sheds a single tear.
I hope no one lives in poverty,
Not a single soul lives feeling lonely.
I dream of no abuse,
Where everyone in society has a use.

I dream of absolute bliss,
This is my one true wish.

Conor Walker (13)
Park High School, Birkenhead

I Have A Dream

I have a dream to walk down a street
And not have to ask for money!
I have a dream not to be beaten for money
Or forced to hand over my belongings!
I have a dream to be in a lovely house
With nice things.
I have a dream to never live on the streets
Or beg for money!
I have a dream that my tummy will always be full
And my purse never empty!
I have a dream that one day there will be no poverty
And no more homelessness!
This is my dream and it keeps me going!

Kerry Keane (14)
Park High School, Birkenhead

I Have A Dream

I have a dream,
To have my family want me back.
Have a good job, without getting the sack.
That people won't always look down at me,
But, if you saw a homeless person, what would you see?

I have a dream,
To sleep in a warm, comfy bed,
But I sleep on the streets instead.
To have a good meal, not a scrap,
Not to get robbed while having a nap.

I have a dream,
To be noticed for being me,
Not how dirty I can be.
I am normal, just alone,
All because I have no home.

Katie Wilson (14)
Park High School, Birkenhead

I Have A Dream

I have a dream
That everything flows like a gentle stream,
No terrorism, racism and no war,
No need to disagree,
Just agree, making the decision together,
Opening the door to a better life
Wherever they may live,
Food, water and some clothes
And a place to sleep;
If we need some water
It's just a walk to the sink,
But to others it's a 10 mile walk
Just to get a drink,
Even if we need food it's
Just a walk to the shops,
But to others they go scavenging
In search of some crops,
This is why I hate the world,
People have so much greed,
Someone who really cares should
Step in and take the lead,
And influence people to give to the poor
And make the world a better place.

Daniel Rainford (13)
Park High School, Birkenhead

I Have A Dream

I have a dream that can only be solved by the present and future,
I hope that citizens of this world can stop being a polluter,
Unity, freedom, pride and joy are a must be,
So the rich and the healthy should give a little TLC,
Poverty is stricken all over the world,
It rises like the tsunami swirled,
Drugs and environmental health are on the up,
But the leaders of this world still haven't done enough,
Blacks and whites are all the same,
We're only human, so why so much pain?
Arm in arm, cheek to cheek, this is what I look to seek,
Racism should be given the red card,
And multiple offenders should be barred,
Bullies in schools beware,
The government is cracking down on it . . . we'll get there,
Theft, violence and wars,
Cause serious damage . . . so obey the laws,
Third World countries are not counted,
That is why we take it for granted,
Resources, materials and products are slim,
For those people who need them, life is very dim,
Child abuse is nothing but a crime,
So listen here to this wonderful rhyme,
This world needs a tutor,
It needs to be shown the meaning of life,
Now it's time to end this poem,
Please take heed and go home knowing that you have done right.
It takes a community to save its people,
But the world to save . . . everything

Stephen McKeown (13)
Park High School, Birkenhead

I Have A Dream

I have a dream
There won't be any child abuse at all,
It's sad that anyone could hurt anyone that small.
Just because they are short, you must be thick
Anyone who could do this has got to be sick.
They haven't done anything at the end of the day,
So please don't let this child abuse stay.
Their small feet and cute face
We need to stand up for this, it's a serious case!
They think they're naughty and very bad,
That's why they think their abusers are so mad.
The children only wish love will appear,
But really inside they're crying a silent tear.
They'll have their thoughts through the rest of time,
What ifs will be running through their minds
They'll never forget the person who made them weak,
Enough to make them not even speak.
So let's get something done and kick child abuse out
Because something needs to be done without a doubt!

Abbi Taylor (13)
Park High School, Birkenhead

I Had A Dream

I had a dream,
It wasn't to be sitting here in a doorway begging for food.
I had a dream,
It wasn't asking other people to spare me some of their change.
I had a dream,
It wasn't eating breakfast, lunch and dinner out of a bin.
I had a dream,
It wasn't full of loneliness.
I had a dream,
It wasn't this; it wasn't my life as it is,
Now it was having a place called home.

Beth Garrity (14)
Park High School, Birkenhead

I Have A Dream

I have a dream,
In that dream I wake up in a warm bed
And not a cold, eerie doorway.

I have a dream,
That I can eat nice food every day,
And not scraps that people throw away.

I have a dream
That I can go for a walk about,
Without feeling ashamed, but I can't.

I have a dream
That I can go to sleep at night without feeling
I would get killed or robbed.

I have a dream
And in that dream I am not homeless,
But that's just a dream;
Dreams don't become reality when you're homeless.

Darren Lloyd (14)
Park High School, Birkenhead

I Have A Dream

I have a dream to . . .

H ave a wonderful and loving family
A mazing car that roars through the wind
V ery expensive clothing that will turn heads
E verything will be wonderful

A nd that would be my dream but instead . . .

D ays drag by in the cold wet winters
R estless nights on floor as hard as stone
E verybody stares, laughs and jokes
A nd I can't even buy a decent meal
M y life is hell and everyone can tell
   I had a dream . . . just a dream!

Alex Lynch (14)
Park High School, Birkenhead

I Have A Dream

I have a dream that my daddy
won't hit me and everything
will be how it used to be.

I have a dream that he will kiss
me goodnight, hug me and love me
and hold me tight.

I have a dream that more of my
daddy's love is showing.
This is my dream and it keeps me going.

Beth O'Donnell (12)
Park High School, Birkenhead

Untitled

I have a dream that when I wake up the world is going to be free
From all the crime in the world.
Bones breaking, people dying from all the crime.
Innocent people get killed and their children
Have to suffer from having no parents.
Hundreds of people are being killed in the world,
Even as I write this poem now.
One day I have a dream that the world will be free from all the crime.
Every time I see people suffering I dream that the world
Will be free from all the crime.
This is not only a dream it is the whole world's dream,
This is not only a dream, it is our everything!
One day I will be one of those people who are being killed by crime.
Crime is even going on in jail.
There are some people who even kill their mothers
And drop out of school.
When I look at the television I see a lot of crime going on,
Not only where I live but in the whole world.
And they kill each other with knives, guns, bricks
And all sorts of things.
So if you believe that this dream will come true,
It will some day if you believe.

Daniel Lecoko (13)
Park High School, Birkenhead

I Have A Dream

I have a dream
to stop all this war,
keep on going and there will be more.

I have a dream
to stop all disease,
everyone's asking, will you just stop it please?

I have a dream
to stop child abuse,
everything we try all goes to use.

I have a dream
to kill slavery,
help the poor by giving some money.

I have a dream
to stamp out racism,
stop all the fighting and let's live as one!

Jordan Allen
Park High School, Birkenhead

I Have A Dream!

I have a dream that violence will go away,
And in this world it will not stay.
I hate to see people cry,
On the news every day someone dies.
It's terrible to live this way,
Let's make it stop so my bad dreams go away.
Domestic violence, drugs and more,
Children left behind closed doors.
Racism is bad enough,
It leaves people sad and feeling rough.
Let's make it stop, let's stand our ground,
Let's get together and make the world go round.

Nicole Hartley (12)
Park High School, Birkenhead

I Have A Dream

I have a dream that the grass was green,
The air was filled with laughter,
No people have to beg for tea,
Forever and ever after.

No more people lying around,
No more bombs have hit the ground,
As the years go by
No more war planes can fly.

What is this dream I am seeing,
That will never come true,
No need in believing,
The sky will never be blue.

I can keep on dreaming,
It will not be true . . .

Cindie Williams (12)
Park High School, Birkenhead

I Have A Dream

I have a dream where the world can be clean,
Not selfish or thoughtless or something that's mean.
All these fumes and gases we know today,
If they all went away we would shout, 'Hooray.'

You know and we know we need a solution,
For this terrible thing we call pollution.
We all need to help
And not think of yourself.

You hear on the news that people are ill,
Makes me sad, I can't keep still.
We know the cause, it's called pollution,
Not yet, still there is no solution.

It damages our world,
We need to stand tall.
This is our world,
Don't let it fall!

Shannon Willoughby (12)
Park High School, Birkenhead

I Have A Dream

I have a dream
For Daddy to be alive,
Not lying under the remains of the Twin Tower once high.

I have a dream
for Mommy to be well,
Not suffering in hospital with an oxygen mask cell.

I have a dream
For my brother to quit,
Not buying all that pot so it can be lit.

I have a dream
For my sister not to fret,
Not threatnin' to be away with herself so that boy can't upset.

I have a dream
For Lucy to come round,
Not being judged on her colour by my neighbourhood crowd.

I have a dream
For Spot to be there,
Not getting kicked in the street so everyone can stare.

I have a dream
For everyone to be here,
To be happy and smiling and close and near . . .

Hannah Amos (12)
Park High School, Birkenhead

I Have A Dream . . .

I have a dream as the years go by
I look up and see no warplanes fly,
Bombs not allowed, smiles all around,
No wounded bodies lying on the ground.

Racism is no longer allowed,
All races can be one crowd,
Laughing between all colours
They can be sisters and brothers.

Pollution is not the answer for getting around,
We can still have cars, solar power has been found,
Factory chimneys not puffing out smoke,
Children can play without needing to choke.

No people on their own living in the streets,
They shall have a bed with covers and sheets,
A smile on their face, food they can eat,
Live in warmth, no having cold feet.

This is my dream as the years go by.

Jemma Edwards (12)
Park High School, Birkenhead

Untitled

I have a dream,
I can wake up and look out my window
And not be hit and shouted at by drunks.
I can act like a normal person.
I don't want to rob and beg for my money,
I would rather work for my money and buy my own food.
People I know from school and old neighbours stare at me,
I hide my face with embarrassment.
I have no money, no clothes, no food, no water,
Things you all take for granted I wish to have.
I have a dream,
Everyone can live and get along with each other.
Violence is the main thing you have to watch out for
On the rough streets,
You don't know when some madman could come
And kick you in your head.
I have a dream,
You can have a nice warm bed,
Somewhere you are sheltered and safe.
A place people can go visit.
The streets are cold, bare, lonely,
Nowhere you can be warm and sheltered.
All the dirty looks and stares.
I think to myself, should I end my life?
Nobody will know, and nobody will care.

Andy Cowan (14)
Park High School, Birkenhead

I Had A Dream

I had a dream that one day
All the people of the world would laugh together
And every face would host a smile.
We'd learn to get through our troubles as a nation,
As a country, as a world, as one.
I had a dream that one day
All the people of the world would laugh together,
And everyone would be given hope.

I had a dream that one day
All the families would forget their differences
And all children would have a mum and dad.
We'd learn to solve our problems together
As friends, as neighbours, as one.
I had a dream that one day
All the families would forget their differences
And everyone would be given love.

I had a dream that one day
The world would be in true harmony
And all the people would suddenly be friends,
We'd forget the prejudice and hate,
As a society, as a community, as one.
I had a dream that one day
The world would be in true harmony.

Then I grew up.

Helen Robb (14)
Polam Hall School, Darlington

I Have A Dream

The other day I had a dream
A dream where everything was so obscene
Bitter rivalry between the same race
They were stupid, blind and a huge disgrace
Others suffered for their crimes
The end of the world was just a matter of time
Powered by evil you wanted and worked hard to get
Some were rich, while others drowned in debt
'Love thy neighbour' was last aside
People of trust made mistakes and lied
Everything was grey and bleak
The fragile planet was getting evermore weak
Very few actually knew or cared
How far the world was from utter despair
However, still I have a vague dream
A dream where everything is as it seems
The dream isn't perfect, to be sure
But it's a thousand times better, and much more pure.
Where the natural order is repaired
And the social group is much more fair
No more denial and no more excuses
Where everyone felt loved and had their uses
Long, lazy days and sweet fun-filled nights
Where I've got you and everything's gonna be alright
With friends who love you and who'll always be there
People who do special things so you know they care
Earth is at peace and everything is good
Life is simple and is as it should
And just as I thought this dream would never end
I woke up and the nightmare started again.

Ella Gainsborough (15)
Prestwich Arts College, Manchester

My Dream Is . . .

My dream is . . .
To grow up
Being a young lady,
Not being so shady,
Having my dream home
And having an ice cream cone,
Getting married,
Moving out,
Having a good laugh about,
But you never know
How it will turn out,
Keep on dreaming
And don't worry about leaving.

Sehrish Yameen (12)
Prestwich Arts College, Manchester

Junior's Death

In my final hours
I think of greater powers,
I think of my feelings
While I'm not healing.

Why was I shot?
Will I be forgot?

I once had a dream
Which is now lost,
I am now paying the
Ultimate cost!

Why was I shot?
Will I be forgot?

Where am I going
And why is it so light?
I can't see through
This great and powerful light.

Why was I shot?
Will I be forgot?

Benjamin Marga Clarke (12)
St Chad's RC High School, Runcorn

Why Bother?

Why do people drop bombs?
Why?
Why do people find it fun?
Why?
Why do people risk their lives to hurt others?
Why?
How can they laugh when people die?
How?
How can they walk away from it with a smile?
How?
How can they be proud?
How?
Do they know it's wrong?
Do they?
Do they think about their own lives?
Do they?
Do they think about their family and friends?
Do they?
How come they can walk away with their heads held high?
How come?
How come they can watch the Earth being destroyed?
How come?
How come they want to kill the Earth and living things?
How come?
Why are they so cold-hearted?
Why?
There must be a reason why?
What is the reason?
Nobody will know why, only the soul within the person.
Some people are kind, but others are cruel.

Shannon Miller (12)
St Chad's RC High School, Runcorn

Imagine

Imagine a world with no war,
    Just peace
Imagine a world with no death,
    Just peace
Imagine a world with no enemies,
    Just peace
Just imagine a quiet world,
    Imagine.

Tony Gerrard (11)
St Chad's RC High School, Runcorn

Racism

There is no need for racism,
No need at all.
People are all the same,
No matter the colour of their skin.
Black and white,
Should all unite in harmony.
Peace will come soon.

Gareth Hewitt (11)
St Chad's RC High School, Runcorn

Why Do We?

Why do we say but don't do?
Why do we give but don't receive?
Why do we take but don't give enough?
Why do we say we don't have enough but we have more than others?
Why do we ask for more when we don't need it?
Why do we take things for granted?
Why are we greedy?
Oh why God, why?

Steven Craig (12)
St Chad's RC High School, Runcorn

Famous Words

Famous words go against all things
Famous words have gone against racism
Famous words have gone against violence

Usually famous words come from famous people

What is the point in racism?
What is the need to hate people?

If I had a dream, the world would see clearly . . .

No racism!
No violence!

Famous words should count!

Anthony Fisher (12)
St Chad's RC High School, Runcorn

What If . . . ?

What if . . .
Black and white people were equal?

What if . . .
People with disabilities were treated equally?

What if . . .
Religion didn't matter?

What if . . .
War was never thought of?

What if . . .
Global warming wasn't happening?

What if . . .
Pollution wasn't an issue?

What if . . .
Bombs were not used to kill?

What if . . .
Children could get along and appearances didn't matter?

What if . . .
We could live as one with peace in the world?

Jessica Harris (12)
St Chad's RC High School, Runcorn

Dream

Dream,
That old people were treated like young people.
Dream,
That all countries would become peaceful.
Dream
That animals were treated like humans.
Dream,
That everybody's religion would be peaceful.
Dream
That everybody fitted in.
Dream,
That all bullying would stop.
Dream,
That terrorism would end.
Dream,
That everybody would be equal.

Tony Dainteth (12)
St Chad's RC High School, Runcorn

Racism Should Stop

Racism is bad
It's no good at all
You don't want to be racist
It can make people sad.

It happens in football
It happens everywhere
We need to put a stop to it
And end it all.

We might not look alike
We might have different religions
We might have different skin colours
But we are all people

We must all bring racism
To an end
A message to all
That people should send.

Joe Bibby (12)
St Chad's RC High School, Runcorn

I Have A Dream

If I had one wish,
We'd be treated all the same
And would be respected equally.

If I had one wish,
Women and men would be shown
The same equal rights.

If I had one wish,
There would be peace
And harmony in the world.

If I had one wish,
Pollution would be stopped,
Animals would not be killed
And terrorism would be brought to an end.

Rebecca Begley (12)
St Chad's RC High School, Runcorn